The Word For Rain Is Rain

by

M. C. Rush

ISBN: 978-81-19654-12-3

First Edition: 2023
Rs. 200/-

Cyberwit.net
HIG 45 Kaushambi Kunj, Kalindipuram
Allahabad - 211011 (U.P.) India
http://www.cyberwit.net
Tel: +(91) 9415091004
E-mail: info@cyberwit.net

Printed at Repro.

These are the grains I got
when I grabbed at the sand.

Contents

The Experiment

Run a brain through life,
then drain it of what it learned of good
and use this elixir to begin again.

The Method

First we must define our terms.
Then we must disclose our premises and assumptions.
Then we must propose our hypothesis.
Then we must examine and test the evidence.
Then we must formulate our conclusion
using irrefutable fact and sound logic.
Then we must do whatever our instincts and desires
drove us to do from the beginning.

If I am a leaf
on the stream of consciousness,
does that imply a tree?
Does it imply a sea?

What I Found 3

Digging after a rain under an ancient tree
I found a rusty sword blade.

Cleaning it with a lemon and steel wool
I found a poem engraved into the metal.

Reading the words, reading them again,
I found enlightenment.

The next time it rained
I buried the blade beneath a young sapling.

Every spring is spring,
but only my spring was my spring.
Summer, fall, winter, too.

His Work

Man, upon seeing the world,
grabbed its nose and broke it off.

It looks better to me thus, he said,
admiring his work.

I no longer believe
in other people.
They are a rumor.
They are a story.
They are a lie.
They won't like me
saying so.
Now I'm free
not to care.

Beautiful

beautiful were the things we saw
beautiful were the things we touched
beautiful the things we took
beautiful the things we made
beautiful the things we sold
beautiful the lies
the pain
loss after beautiful loss—
who could bear such beauty?

a houseboat
on a castle moat
searching for sea,
a sail, and a breeze

My Mind

My mind goes everywhere it can.
And wonders about those places
it doesn't know or cannot find.
That is my mind.

How Many

How many of the necessary things have you acquired?
How many of the necessary understandings have you achieved?
How many of the necessary acts have you undertaken?
How many of the necessary commitments have you made?

Have you even learned what "necessary" means?

Laughing

To avoid the void,
self looks at self.

Unaware of the void,
world never looks at world.

What is that sound
that sounds so much like laughing?

I am drunk
on the idea of myself.
Who is drunk?
No idea.

Sure

Drunk, though I didn't drink.
Blind, though I didn't blink.
Sure, though I didn't think.
Drowned, though I didn't sink.

The barking at night
of an unknown dog
heard
must be answered,
or the dark echo
will din your day.

I Just Have To

I am not what I am
I say
again and again.
I'm what I was.
I just have to
get back to myself.
Get out of the way.

Multiverse

Each of us is a universe
that carries the world within its mind.
It dies and dies and dies
and is renewed:
what is this world?
What is this mind?

Here, have one taste.
And never again.

Now long for it,
pine for it,
forever.

The Solution to the Mind-Body Problem

Zero.

You are born on the ground
craving stars
you cannot reach.
You suffer, you suffer.
You climb.

Willful Innumeracy

How many of the three-and-a-half billion
could have been the one?
Or, more accurately, one?
I have to believe none.
I have to believe none.

The left hand was made for this,
the right for that,
but the eyes were made for everything.

The Names 2

How many names in this world
did I learn?

How many names in this world
did I never learn?

How many have I forgotten?

How many have I tried to forget?

How many things in this world
have names?

How many do not?

How soon we become ourselves.

And, having done so,
how quickly we begin to lose ourselves.

To Think

Once I learned a few of the names
I wanted all the names,
to think with.

But the few I got were only names,
and the thoughts only thoughts.

And then I forgot
the names, and the joy
in knowing.

To Another Poet

You want to talk
endlessly
about yourself.

I want to make
charms and invocations,
powerful and eternal.

Poetry is big enough
for you to do your thing
and me, mine.

I would rather delight in the world
than anything
than anything
than anything else.

I Got This

Today I got this—small bliss!
I didn't get that, or the other thing
I had wanted—what of it?

If what is impossible is best,
how shall we ever be contented
only with what can be?

Every Day 2

Kill yourself
by doing something differently,
by doing something you've never done,
something you've never seen anyone do.

Give birth
to someone who will have done that thing,
someone who claims to be you,
but isn't, is better, is new.

From how many angles must we see a thing
to know anything about that thing?

Always one more.

The Secret of Antigone

Another challenge from another point of view
needing to assert itself by daring me to defy, to resist,
to sacrifice what seems important for what seems right, but
I am tired of standing up, of standing on my own, standing my
ground, standing for what I want to stand for, dead tired
of doing what I dream into honor, alone, surely asleep—yet,
not to? Not to think, not to feel, not to act? How, how,
even when the result is a yard spread with remains?

I want everything to be
interesting and lovely,
but I'm not sure my desire
is either.

Maybe

If everything is relative,
then relativity, being a thing, is relative.

Rules don't scale well.

I am absolutely uncertain.

If you must be sure, don't be.
If you must see, beauty.
If you must, you're lost.

Sanity

No one
is sane.

We
couldn't be,

living every moment
under threat.

Why pretend
we can't see the end?

The Neighbor

The neighbor is shouting
through the wall.
So angry. So intolerable.
Take them away
and leave me here.
Or leave them and take me.
We cannot coexist.

Words Before An Absent Crowd

Admire what I've said.
Or admire that I said it.
Or that I set out to be admired.
Now I'm tired.
Still inspired,
just less willing to commit
my life to the half-dead.

The world betrays you
until you forget how to love it.

Then it rejoices,
I suppose?

I have never forgotten
any love.
This is why I never married.
Nothing beats marriage
for extinguishing love.
Better to lose every love
than to feel one die inside.
Better to embrace a ghost
than its corpse.

Isn't It

Isn't it great
how we reiterate?

When we have so little
we must recycle.

What we were back when
we'll be again.

Over and over
like obstinate clover.

Say that something is happening.
Do you have a right to change it?
Do you have a right not to?

Substitute "responsibility" for "right"
and read this again.

The Trap 2

What rights, what consideration,
are due the trap
that you have stumbled into?

To what is that
which interferes entitled?

That which impedes,
that which thwarts—
what villain would deny it
recognition and recompense?

All The Hearts

All the hearts I met were encrypted.

With what pity their owners regarded me
when I couldn't decode them!

To paint the moon blue.
And then yellow. And then red.
And then (don't forget!) white again.

Never keep anything
or it may become precious:
then it keeps you.

Analysis 2

What we want to see clearly
we separate from—
what we want to know clearly
we investigate—
what we want to feel clearly
we embrace—
hilarious!

Revealed

Someone approaches, or you watch them from afar—
do you want them to succeed or wish them to fail?

Here is your mirror, and here is your selfie:
what you think is what you are.

This is the poem that's not good enough.
It's partial, unsatisfying—it's rough.
Let's leave it, then, move on to better stuff.

The Order of Things

I saw her.
I loved her.
I saw that I loved her.

Lost Appetite

There was a thing
I thought to eat,

I checked it out
and took a bit.

I tasted it
and thought it sweet,

but now I know
that it was shit.

Listening

Listening to you speak
from the other side of the wall;
that you will never speak of me
matters not at all;
I listen for the song,
not for the call.

The Three

The one who knows is a fraud.
The one who doesn't know is a fool.
The one who doesn't want to know
is unforgivable.

Something or Nothing

Where there is something, take something.
Where there is nothing, seek something.
If, despite seeking, you find nothing,
be content with nothing.

What there is, you are not responsible for.
What there isn't, even less so.
If you are something, rejoice!
If you are not, rejoice!

Which Came First

Are the destruction and the disappointment separate?
If so, which came first?
Or are they somehow the same thing?
Was this inevitable from the start?
Or did it—did I—go horribly wrong
somewhere along the way?
Would it have been better never
to have lived to see this?
Or is there fulfillment in witness?

π

You give me pi to two places,
but I asked for pi to a hundred places,
a thousand.

If the difference is not significant,
why not comply
with my wishes?

I will of course comply,
if what you expect is that I should lie.
But why, but why, but why?

The Scarf

You wove a scarf
of insincerity and deficiency
and wrapped it around my throat:
I choked.

Absolutely 2

You wake
and suddenly have unearned power
over others.

Of course you use it
until you lose it.
There's too much at stake.

Never trust
one who says
Not lust.

Love is fine
if it is real,
and so is wine.

Best touch today
what tomorrow
will take away.

Middle Age Mantra

You would have loved me
if you'd known me
before I became
this half-dead thing
I practice saying
in a mirror.

The ocean is constantly moving
into the sky, and falling.

We are constantly moving
into the world, and falling.

Love or truth, you ask?
Is love true? Always? Ever?
Dare we love the truth?

What starts off beautiful and strong
withers and weakens.
Love will evolve into pity.

Comes The Day

There comes the day when it would no longer be safe to make you divine,
when the anger and the righteous thirst for vengeance grow too large,
tilt the scale of your personality and your humanity into Old Testament
territory, away from the ennobling love of all things.

Disqualified, do you embrace your life as a petty, impetuous ape,
or do you retreat into daydreams of the past's futures?

AI Think, Therefore AI Am

AIs are the gods we've always dreamed of,
for better and for worse.

What is more human than to build a god
and then subject oneself to it?

Many worry that we won't build it well enough
to bequeath it our values, our priorities.

I worry only that we won't build it well enough
to improve upon them.

Of Love & Trust

Let me drink from a coconut, eat spicy shrimp,
and feel the cooling breeze from the sea on my skin.

I love the day. I love the night.
I trust the dusk more than the dawn.

The poets I don't like are the ones
who don't tell me anything I want to know.

Or, Do As You Will

Sit there, near.
Don't speak.
Don't refrain from speaking.
Breathe without sighing.
Smile, smile.
Look at me.
Vanish.

Empty

What to think,
if infinity is mostly empty?

Is it empty like a blank canvas
or like a dead brain?

Could it be both?
And how much does it matter?

We 2

The things we want most, we can't have.
The things we can have, we can't keep.

What we keep are illusions,
and they are disappointing and unsatisfying.

Who are we, compelled to live
in an impossible way?

Those who broke it
should pay for it.

Those who found it broken
should see to it.

Say a new thing
or say an old thing
better.

I radiated joy toward everyone
till someone made me feel bad for it.

Now, like the moon,
I only shine when shone on.

Standing on one foot
in the storm—
sure to fall, but when?

Arete

Neither predators nor prey have honor.
Nor require it to restrain their worst impulses.
What are we, that need a code to guide us?

Did I—
I must have done—
but did I really
once think of others
without this spontaneous upwelling
of disappointment and dismay?
What was I then?
O, what am I now?

Pas de Deux

Look at conviction
separated into weather.

Look at weather
guessed at like the future.

Look at the future
abandoned like conviction.

Close your eyes.
Do you hear me?

Almost All of It

Every day millions do what I would never do.
Are they more human, or less?
Every day I do what millions never will, or would.
Who are they? Who am I?
Every day I think it matters less, all of it.

A Word Like That

You can't use a word like *ressentiment* in a poem,
no one said to me one day while I was minding my own business.
You're not man enough. You don't have enough degrees.
You haven't paid your dues. Who do you think you are?
What are you trying to prove? You'll never get away with it.
Why do you always set out to alienate everybody?
What'd they ever do to you? Don't do it. *Don't you do it!*
Nobody ranted, and swore, and raged.
And I chuckled, nodded, and put pen to page.

I said yes and love said no
so I said fine then
I'm gonna go

Yes and No 2

The world said yes.
Then the people said no.

Damn the people
who noed my yes!

Truths

Grab a truth.
Grab another.
Truths are soap bubbles
floating by on false breezes,
each beautiful
and ready to pop.

Every bee believes
what she needs
will be in the next
blossom.

She isn't wrong
until she's wrong.

Again 8

If it's worth saying once it's worth saying again.
If it's worth saying once it's worth saying again.
If it's worth hearing once it's worth hearing again.
If it's worth hearing once it's worth hearing again.
But how shall and how should we determine worth?
But how shall and how should we determine worth?

Burn!

Burn, if you are going to burn!
What point delaying a flame?
Kindling is best when it is fresh.
Will you be mostly smoke,
fire, or ash?
The thing about heat is it cannot last.
Why wait?

The Character of the Age

Charmless, humorless,
profligate, irresponsible,
trivial, petty, and cruel.

How could the world
hear my great suffering?

It is quieter
than a raindrop in the grass.

Commemoration

Topple all statues,
remove all monuments.
Let no one be remembered
so long as we must die.

Love Is

Love is the briefest thing,
like an insect that lives to bite
a bite that torments
and then, spent, dies.

Love is the longest thing,
like a star that burns for eons
only to find, as it finally fades,
that the darkness remains unlit.

How much
of what came before
must we tear down
to build what we need?

How much
of what we build
will survive
the next generation?

Everything
costs too much.

I'll buy
no more.

Let freedom
ring.

What would have been enough
was evidently too much.
What would have been enough?

Al Final

I miss
everything I've missed,

ache
for what I never knew,

dream
of all I couldn't imagine.

The Self 2

I remember
when I remembered
what I remember
for the first time.

In that moment only
did I live truly.

What do you call the ghost
of a ghost of a ghost?
The self.

I have been
as I have been
for as long as I have been.

How else could I have been?

Any other
would have been another.

I had my reasons.
My reasons no longer apply.
Now what do I have?

Knowing

To be lost
you must have some idea
of where you're meant to be—
maybe they're right,
maybe it's better to know nothing.
But I'm committed now.
If all I can know
is that I can't know it,
then I will know that.

Contained within
the infinity cavern:
oblivion.

Sacrifice

No one wanted
what I had.

Nothing will take it.
Nothing will take it

all
in the end.

Yesterday you were that.
Today you are this.
Tomorrow you will be
unknowable.

Alone 3

I have done so much
unnoticed.

I have given so much
to no one.

Next time
I will walk through an empty world
and never know what it is
to be alone.

I did what I did.
I didn't do what I didn't do.
What more is there to say?

Shh

What have I not said?
What will I not say?

Perhaps the time of quiet,
long-approaching, nears.

Let everyone shout now—
what can I contribute to that?

Everyone wants to be a mouth,
not an ear. So, okay.

Every voice combines
to say no more,
so, no more.

After

What if this is the best
that could be made
with what was left?

Would it, could it,
then, be enough?

The most fortunate
see much change but little loss
during their lives.

Bard

sundrum
moonlute
windflute
and rainhorn

running
alone under stars
singing to myself
of non-eternal renewal

Something 4

Something is amiss,
something is awry;
something just like this—
something is a lie!

Laissez les bon temps roulez

Indulge. Enjoy.
Grab a little as it goes by.
It's almost gone.
And so are you.

The Obstacles

Happily I evaded my obstacles
in the dim light, so they began
to hit me, knock me down,
pin me.

Now, with little blood left,
I doze, and daydream
of the days of maneuverability,
the days of dance,
those days of freedom.

And Die

Learn everything and die.
Learn nothing and die.
Laugh and die.
Cry and die.
Win, lose, and die.

Warm autumn rain.
How many times?
How many more?

I need this.
That, and the next thing.
I lack, I lack, I lack.
I have been moved into a position
of non-acquisition.
Imprisoned in want.
Can't they relent,
reverse the loss?
I need this.

What Else 2

If I influenced others
as others have influenced me…
but I influence no one.

If others loved me
as I have loved others…
but others don't love me.

To continue to welcome
the influence of others who don't love me…
what else?

From the Manure of Ideology

Reap the crop,
inter the stalk,
and plant again.

Enough for a taste
will never sate.
The eating is best
if you don't always eat.
Fast! Feast!
Feast! Fast!
Have dessert
neither first nor last.

Watch someone
watching themselves.

Watch yourself
watching someone
watching themselves.

Do you see?

Why?

Why embrace a reflection?
Because that is all we can reach.

Why embrace a shadow?
Because it embraces back.

Why embrace a dream?
Because the night is long and lonely.

Why embrace a lie?
Don't! Don't! Don't!

Judgment Day 2

Look what all the petty little people have done.
Look what all the stupid little people have allowed.
To hell with them. To hell with all of them.

The Future 5

Everything flattened.
Everything blended.
Everything reduced.
Simplified.
Consolidated.
Ruined.
Abandoned.
Forgotten.

The Contradiction

What I say here
I will reject here,
and return to here
and embrace again
while yet embracing
the contradiction.

The Worst Habit

The worst habit,
the most damaging,
is to associate
with the unworthy.

And who is unworthy?
bleat those who know best.

I enjoyed it
but it was not enough.
A taste. A tease.
Too brief
to take seriously.

Still we are allowed
to make a little magic
where none care to look.

Desire 3

A lifetime to more closely study
the sublime yin-yang
of indulgence and restraint.

Give enough,
but not what you will
suffer for the lack of.

To not be
is the easiest thing of all.

To contemplate it—
impossible.

Each pecan, falling, finds a place
to land on the grass,
but position doesn't last.

Sculpture

The weathered ruin of the cliff,
worn by wind, by rain,
seems beautiful in its shape,
with its serrated edge—
but what did it look like
when it was new, undegraded?
We don't know.

A Warning

To want something beyond reason,
almost beyond tolerance,
is a warning that you are at risk
of being overwhelmed, subverted.
Heed it, or don't. But hear it.

It is easy to say nothing.
It is easy to say something.
Much harder to say the right thing.
Harder still to mean it.

Speak to now?
Or speak to always?
Anyway, speak.

Some People 2

Some people love people
instead of religion or politics,
instead of art or books,
instead of war or sports,
instead of television or poems.

How the hell do they do it?

If things look bad, take a step back.

If they still look bad, take another step back.

Keep stepping back
until you can see things
differently.

The reproductive drive
says *Me! Mine!*

I say this without joy or pride:
Life evolves to genocide.

Is this the one?
I don't know.
Is this the one?
I'll probably never know.
This one?
Most likely, none of them.
So…fine.
Do I continue
or do I stop?

Think what you want to think.
Believe what you want to believe.
Say what you want to say.
Do what you want to do.
Be…what you are.

Do it. Don't do it.
Soon it won't matter.

If it doesn't matter then,
does it matter now?

Failure 3

I take
everything I have become

I try
to make of it
everything I was

If you want to be loved,
be attentive.
If you want to be loved,
be kind.
If you want to be loved,
love.
If you want to be loved.

Live if you can.
Die if you must.
Why involve the world?

The Spoon

To really enjoy someone's poetry,
you have to quit trying to make
more or less of it than it is.
It is.
Love it or leave it.
Don't look for your own sweet face
in the bowl of the spoon.

The Wind 3

If it's a god in a cloud,
then I embrace the god.
If it's a devil in the rain,
then I embrace the devil.
If it's death in the wind,
then I embrace…the wind.

Wind, rain, cloud—
or is it the embracing
that defines me?

War 3

Choose a side,
then look across the drawn line
at yourself, defiant,
shielding another position.

The Gavel to the Gallows

It is easy to pardon the innocents—
and we should—
but what of the foolish, the gullible,
the easily-swayed irrationals?
Should we judge them, sentence them,
the same as the malicious,
the same as the unethicals?
And if not, what, then,
do we do with them?

Nowhere in the world
is big enough for me.

I don't think the world
is big enough for me.

How big I must be!

One man's surrealism is another's realism.
Do you choose the lens or the prism?
You have two eyes.

Better Poetry

Which makes better poetry,
the school of fish,
the hungry shark,
or the sinuous, sonorous octopus?

The Meaning

There is the meaning that there is,
and then there is the meaning that emerges
when I shuffle words.

Are the things society celebrates most
inherently absurd or made absurd
by the embrace?

Turn this way, sadness.
Turn the other way, disappointment.
Where, again, did I once see joy?

Gnostic Acrostic

What if, in a primordial war,
horribly, the wrong god won
and then convinced all of us
that he was what he was not?
Imagine every subsequent soul,
forever duped, perpetually lost.

The Way 3

The way is not the way.
The way is not the way to the way.

The way is the is not
and is not the is.

The not-the-way may be more important
than the way.

But you will focus on the way
and, in so doing, lose the way.

That's just the way of it.

Glimpse

the glow through the trees on the snow in the dark
the touch of the pain from the thought of the past
the beep of the machine by the side of the bed

The Most Impossible Challenge

to make
of your life
a beautiful
poem

No names!
I want to know you,
not your name.
And mine will only
mislead you about me.
Don't remember—
see!

the world didn't perform—the duet failed—silence

In Which Direction

Those who are happy will be unhappy.

But will those who are unhappy be happy?

In which direction will the butterfly flit
when it departs the flower?

Do I?

Do I perceive, or only believe that I perceive?
Do I realize, or only believe that I realize?
Do I know, or only believe that I know?
Do I understand, or only believe that I understand?
Do I remember, or only believe that I remember?

Do I believe, or only believe that I believe?

The Journey

Some go away, away, away,
but not all make the journey.

Some come back, back, back,
but not all complete the journey.

Some get lost, lost, lost,
but they, at least, understand the journey.

And, they say, you mustn't mourn
your beautiful hair. It isn't there.
You're grieving but you're still
breathing—and that's something.
We must settle for achievements now
dwarfed by those we dreamed of then.
Never mind what's fair. Have you
discovered all the new ways to fail?
You will.

In My Yard

The pine needles fall to the ground.
The sycamore leaves fall on the pine needles.
I walk on the sycamore leaves.

Advice 8

Look closely. Look again
until you are watching.
Watch until you see.

A spider on its web,
me in my thoughts,
awaiting intrusion.

sound of crow
is a different crow than
sight of crow

All your troubles
are less trouble
than one of mine.

Our Story

We look but don't see.
We listen but don't hear.
We think but don't understand.
We feel but don't act.
We live but don't live.

Our story of ourselves
is just a story, not a self.

Black-eyed Susans
watch me relentlessly
but cannot follow
when I leave.

Strange 3

Everyone is a stranger to me.
Isn't that strange?

Irony Is Always An Error

I rest my hand
on a broken tombstone
on this January day
and feel warmth.

The Word For Rain Is Rain

Between one rain and another
I only know the word for rain.

The Waterfall

The waterfall insists you hear
its music only.

What I Want 6

I want to see again
everything I have seen.

I want to do again
everything I have done.

I want to have again
everything I have had.

But mostly I want to want again
everything I have wanted.

I have lived beside a freeway
and a railroad track.
Now I live next to a cemetery.

What is happening outside?
What is happening inside?

I would like to know
what is happening.

What I used to know
was very nearly enough
for who I used to be.

Those who saw, died.
Those who never did, died.
Death doesn't care.

What is measured changes.
How we measure it changes.
The changes are difficult to measure.

The world takes no responsibility.
The world accepts no blame.
Why should I?

Reasons 2

They come
for reasons of their own.

They leave
for reasons of their own.

I have opinions
of their reasons.

Other Things

I look at all the things
others have done
and seek to do those things
and other things.

Suffering is long
and joy so short,
and the worst people
believe this inevitable.

Why do I do what I do
and not do what I don't do?
Why am I the kind to ask?

The King of Crows

Put me in a castle
on a mountaintop
in an eternal blizzard.

Warm inside,
with everything I need—
an ecstasy of rejection.

The King of Crows
smiling
at the falling snow.

When I think of you now
all I can feel is pain.

But when I think of you now
all I can think is "Thank you."

And suddenly what a moment before would have been trivial,
forever impossible.

When it's gone—
when it's taken,
when it's lost,
when it's given up—
ask "What next, then?"

Context 2

Everything seems more meaningful
when it's part of a larger conversation.

But it's all just talk.

I Didn't Understand

I didn't understand what I had when I had it.
I didn't understand what I lost when I lost it.
I didn't understand what I didn't understand.
Understand?

What will never be
shines equally
with the illusion of possibility.

Inattention
is the murderer
of every treasure.

I see that everything matters.
I see that nothing matters.
I see that seeing is being.

Afraid of yesterday, run to the future.
Afraid of tomorrow, run to the past.
Fearing both, race in circles until dead.

Basho Corrected

The stupid frog
falls into the dark pond:
silence.

when strength becomes weakness
when joy becomes pain
when hope becomes horror
then
then

And so,
just another
failure,
a concatenation
of bad decisions,
a juxtaposition
of joy and regret,
of hope and disappointment.

Everything is a test,

or

the only test is
realizing that everything is not a test.

Much is gone.
But much remains.
Can less ever again be enough?

If nature and nurture,
what of desire, what of intent?

How much say did I have
in what I became?

My Critique

Everything can be criticized.
But maybe not everything should be criticized?

I think I will criticize
the habit of criticizing.

And then, perhaps, probably,
I will criticize my critique.

Wham! Pow! Slam!
He goes down.
He won't get up again.
The view from the ground is
so many anonymous feet
marching desperately
in every direction.

And for me,
my circumstances having been foreseen,
a voice said,
"Let him be full of venomous spiders,
let him be full of angry bees."
And so it was.

We look at the self to see
what lies behind it.
To see what lies.

What good the thing
that knows no other thing,
that needs no other thing?

The Lens 2

The world has things.
People have stories of things.
It's exhausting, eventually,
seeing everything filtered
through the lens of interpretation.
The world has people,
but people don't have the world.

This, too, is a story.

Has anything
ever
equalled
the horror
perpetrated
by humanity
on everything?

Humans 2

Humans, seeing the beauty of the world,
work night and day
to turn it into something
they won't miss
when they die.

Autobiography 2

I was huge
with what-I-may-become;
then smaller, smaller,
as possibility dwindled.

Noli Me Tangere

Reality precedes dreams,
and then dreams destroy reality.
—Kim Sŭng-Hŭi, "Sun Mass"

Have we loved well? Can anyone tell?
—Mark Nepo, "Is There Any Other Question?"

What I have held onto
has become what I hold—
I am old! I am old!

My dreams are dreams
I dreamed before—
is there…is there no more?

All my love is then
though I must live just now—
but *how*? *How*? And *how*?

If Only 2

If only we had been better than we were.
What we might have accomplished!

If only we had been wiser, less foolish.
What we might have had!

If only we had loved better than we did.
What we might have become!

The Poetry of the Smoke

Too many poets
say too much.

I'd rather watch the smoke
quietly rising
from the earth
up to the sky.

The poet brings
wisteria into your garden,
kudzu to your office.

Unreasonable

the literal-minded
making myth
of the poet's metaphor

What I couldn't see
until you showed me:
disloyalty.

I asked the Immortal
to tell me the Answer
but died while he was clearing his throat.

Life Unto Death

The question is no question.
The answer is no answer.
Yet I will ask
until silenced.

Let me argue
with the words
that define and constrain
expression.

At the Speed of Light

God, if he existed,
would have been what exploded
in the Big Bang.

He would be as far from us
as it was possible to be,
and getting farther every instant.

You act like hope
is voluptuous

but I find it
frigid

and your act
repulsive.

In darkness
I opt for dreams.
And you?

isn't it
perfect

look listen
touch feel

don't think!

isn't it

I die.

You remember me.

Your memories of me are you,
not me.

I am gone.

Even when I was here
was I here,
since I was mostly
my memories of myself?

There is need.
There is affection.
There is lust.
There is obsession.
But is there love?

We sculpt in marble, in bronze, in memory,
what should be shaped in snow, failing
to see that the differences between them are illusory.

Effrontery

I have envisioned the fall of empires
to accommodate my slightest whim,
the rearrangement of galaxies
to oblige my aesthetic sense.

And yet this pebble has dared
to stub my toe, this puddle
has soaked my sock!

The Letters

I read all the letters,
one set twenty years old,
the other thirty.

How did their authors
change so much
and me not at all?

The Result 2

The first time I did not succeed.
Then I tried and tried and tried.
Then I failed and failed and failed.
Then I died.

Best Days

What I want is to be happier than ever before.
Why should my best day be necessarily behind me?
I need to be able to wake up every morning
thinking *this* might be the best day yet.
Not that it will be for sure, but that there's a chance.
But my last best day was so long ago.
My last best everything.
I'm not ready to walk backwards to the end.
I just want more good days that have a chance at best.

Next time,
fewer books,
more people.

Or more books,
fewer people.
Either will work.

My Advice

I advise you to ignore all advice
and just wing it – wing it in the wind –
be blown – go – arrive – leave – go again –
confront each confrontation with invention
and with glee – move – move – feel –
release – love it till you learn to stop
loving it – fly – fall – be.

Occasionally I suspect
that trees are not worthy
of my unconditional love.

This changes nothing.

The Talisman

I was promised a talisman
that would allow me to leave
the Dying Realm,
but it was a lie.
The lie was the talisman,
and now I have this lie
that I was given
and wonder what I am
to do with it.

The moon is cold
and your heart was cold
and now when I see the moon
I think of your heart.

Then I turn and see
the fiery spray
of the Milky Way.

Everything and Nothing 2

The individual is everything and nothing.
Society is everything and nothing.
Species is everything and nothing.
Life is everything and nothing.
Matter and energy are everything and nothing.
Time and space are everything and nothing.
Everything is nothing; nothing, everything.

What They Will Wonder

How did they know so much, they will ask,
and choose so poorly?
Were their hearts darker than ours?
Did they rejoice in the breaking of things?
Were death and destruction their gods?
Was futility their poetry?

I loitered,
thinking to miss my bus,
but it was waiting for me
as soon as I stepped into the street.

What in sapience obligates?
Am I not as the rest of nature is?
To what does understanding compel me?

People Are In The World

People are in the world,
and then they're not.

We each get our fifteen minutes,
and then we're not.

Dance! Sing!
Or not.

From one thing,
all things.

From all things,
no thing.

From no thing,
one thing.

Without

Without fear
no Christianity.

Without suffering,
no Buddhism.

Without pain,
no medicine.

Without ignorance,
no science.

The Dubious Promise

Hope, torment me not!
But maybe…
…and it's almost impossible,
so why should I hear it?

If there be no truth to tempt me,
then let me empty myself
of the extraneous lie.
Let me try.

With Words

Put down your weapons
if you want to enter through my door.

I see you on my porch
red-faced and breathing heavily.
Find words, find words or go away.

I have food and drink,
I have conversation.
Put down your weapons,
come with words and I'll let you in.

Can you love the snow
while remaining indifferent
to a single flake?

Today

Come to me yesterday's tomorrow;
leave me tomorrow's yesterday.
Let today be an entirety
in which love is love is love
and we live in awe of it.

Remember the highest peak
of love you ever reached?
Love everything like that.

Self-Cultivation

Perhaps the rumors are false.
Perhaps I am not meant to love everyone.
People's pettiness is so repulsive.
People's unwillingness to behave admirably.
Perish the impulse to love the self-loathing.
Perish it again when it rises again.

What was is not:
that is the source of all regret.

The Three Stages

1. Delight
2. Disappointment
3. Death

Everyone you don't like will die.
Everyone you do like will die.
Everyone you love will die.

You may die,
but you'll never have to know it.

Don't fear death. Hate it.

Angry Shades

The memories we carry
can be roused, can protest
inside us.

When they rage
it's best to let them
just have their say
and pass again
to yesterday.

To be alive
is to be upset
about something.
Calm is a dream.

A Totally Different Thing

Where there was something
now there is nothing
but a memory of it,

and that's a totally different thing.

It's not going to go well, they say.
It's not going to end well, they say.
And you think *But it will be different for me.*
Because what else are you going to think?

I ask myself questions
to hear my answers—
why else?

I answer myself
to provoke more questions—
why else?

Every morning
a little less,
and still, the sun.

Death, I see you.
I see where you are not.
What you are not.
What I am.
You are simply
the lack of me.

The Books

Having written his name
in the Book of Mischief,
he spent the rest of the day reading
the Book of Inquiry.

More. And more and more.
Then less and less.
I miss more.

Heart

Hate it?
Hunt it,
then hurt it,
then haunt it.

The Finite 2

If you can count it,
you can't count on it.

It's You

It's not what you are, it's what you do.
It's not what you do, it's what you think.
It's not what you think, it's what you feel.
It's none of these things, it's all of them.
It's you, backgrounded by world.
It's you, remembering previous-you,
building next-you until not-you.

Justice would be easy:
anything we do to another
should immediately be done to us.
But who would wish for that?

What We Want 3

truth
and comfort after truth
and hope after truth
and a larger truth
that heals what truth wounds

Ikigai 2

Bless those
who express the message
of the darkness

But I am a firefly
blinking my little light
until extinguished

We suffer
then stop.

Those we leave behind
suffer then stop.

The cycle repeats
again and again.

From that,
all this.

What you spend
to love
is self.

Having seen
that girl
wearing
that dress,
now I wait
for death
to close my eyes.

Be Delighted

Look at everything and be delighted.
Listen to everything and be delighted.
Feel everything and be delighted.
Consider everything and be delighted.
Discover everything and be delighted.
Lose everything

We think at first
that the superpower
is to speed things up;
later we know
it is to slow.

Make everything last ten times longer.
Imagine the orgasm.
Imagine the stubbed toe.
Imagine the realization
that everything is over.

What I Want 4

A day
that doesn't bring me
closer to death.

The Same Thing

You want the same thing, again,
but differently than you've ever had it.
So many other things—you don't want them.
Your wanting is the same as it ever was.
Where is that one thing, described differently,
displayed in a different light, from a different angle,
disguised, that once more you are looking for?
The next unique iteration of intermittent identity
that you are living for?

After The Apocalypse

Life still strives,
but no one has to hear it
celebrate its cleverness,
complain about its shortfalls,
or anticipate the bloody apocalypse.

Pop

I have inflated a bubble in the world,
filled it with over 5500 poems,
and one day soon
it will pop.

Advice 7

If you must write,
only write what is important enough
to write on the skin of the one you love most
after you have carefully removed it
from what was once their body.

I have never known one person
in this world.

And not for lack of crying.

How It Was Settled

I will not have a husband who would do this,
she said.

I will not have a wife who would do that,
he said.

And so it was settled.

And everyone lived a little while longer
and then died.

In This Life

What is the saddest thing in this life?
Two people trying desperately to like each other
and failing.

What is the best thing in this life?
Two people trying desperately to like each other
and succeeding.

How Far It Spreads

Poetry is like grass, not like trees.
It flourishes but does not endure.
It offers color, not shade.
Like life, it is all one thing,
differently expressed.
We think we tame it in our yard;
we do not see how far it spreads
in word we call weed.

Man shouts "I am apart from nature,"
and nature would laugh
if man weren't the part of nature
evolved for laughing.

The Next

Every moment, a new movement; or
every movement, a new moment.

Bring me the new and let me know it.

Then let me transcend (abandon) it,
moving to the next nexus.

I am a prism attached to a funnel.

I would consume the entirety of eternity—
who will teach me not to destroy what I borrow?

What I Want From Poetry

What I want from poetry is not a reflection of life—
when I want life, I go to life!

What I want from poetry is a fine facet of death,
a fractal aspect of the isn't that is,

for I cannot go there and return
to reflect upon the experience.

A Way 3

There is a way.
Though many have looked
no one has found it.
Though many are looking
no one will find it.
There is a way,
but what good is it?
It is no good.
It simply is.

Woken
by whisper

then back to sleep
in the silence.

Internet 2

We dreamed a renaissance
of connection.

We got an apocalypse
of division.

Others, it seems,
had different dreams.

The Ones I Love

Who would I have loved
ten thousand years ago?

Who would I love
ten thousand years from now?

Those are the ones
I will love today.

Here 5

Here, on this ancient site
where sun and rain have come
so many times for so very long,
I stand for an instant
and say hello-goodbye.

What I have
is what I made
of what I saw.

The Three Stages of Grief

1. Birth
2. Life
3. The Anticipation of Death

Song 2

Either I want to see it rain on the moon
or I want to *make* it rain on the moon,
and you really ought to know which it is
before you enter the dust of my bed where
the gravity is less than anywhere else on earth
and light is infinite but broken into brilliant specks
and spread across the greater infinity of void,
sings the mouth of the moth, kissing
the first flash it finds in the darkness.

In The Rain

Stand out in the rain,
head tilted back, eyes closed.

What more can I possibly tell you?
What more could you possibly ask me?

The longer you stand there,
the less you need to know.

Simple Wish

Give me a full moon
and a small lagoon
on which float
fifty tiny fires.

A pile of sand,
and an entire night
to contemplate the light.

Does the rain remember
dissolving the rock
as it falls again to earth?

If a star lit with every birth
and a star went out with every death,
THEN I might believe in humanity.

Where Is The One

Where is the one who will look for me?
I see the tilted crescent moon.

Where is the one who will speak for me?
I hear the noncommittal wind.

Where is the one who will stand with me?
Here's another wave, perishing on the sand.

Who I Am

I know I am supposed to say I've changed,
but I have not changed.
I am as I always was.
It seems I may always be.
Don't expect an apology.
This is who I am—this is me.

My Life 2

I have had a tangerine.
I have had a mangosteen.
Most everyone who's ever lived
envies me.

Those 2

Those who were faithful now lie dead.
Those who lied, cheated and stole now lie dead.
Those who spoke up, those who remained quiet.
Those who took it and those who didn't.
Those who created, those who destroyed.
Those who helped and those who harmed.
Those are dead and gone forever.
What remains is this world they made,
and those of us who yet inhabit it.

I give up.
I've had enough.
Bring on the next thing
or bring oblivion.

and then
when it's almost too late
everything
so clear
so beautiful

One Word

Who says these words to me?
Words that scream yes or shout no,
that create worlds or condemn this one?

Where do they originate and how do they come to me?
I think they made me—
I wouldn't be much of anything without them.

I am words and words and words,
and someday, maybe by the time you are reading this,
I will be just one word.

Remember me like you remember
only five words
from the most beautiful poem you ever read.

Something always said no.
Now the whole world says no.
No, no, no.

And still I struggle
with this tiny, insistent yes.

I thought,
if I write a poem
and then die,
it will have been worth it,
it will have meant something.

Have I ever had a sillier thought?

I thought the world needed me.
It doesn't.
All is well.

www.ingramcontent.com/pod-product-compliance
Lightning Source LLC
Chambersburg PA
CBHW022159160726
48282CB00024B/251